THOMAS MORAN

EXPLORER IN SEARCH OF BEAUTY

Thomas Moran in 1871, enroute to the Yellowstone. Photograph (retouched) by William Henry Jackson.

Thomas Moran

EXPLORER IN SEARCH OF BEAUTY

A biographical sketch; an account of the history and nature of *The Thomas Moran Biographical Art Collection* in the Pennypacker Long Island Collection, at the East Hampton Free Library, New York; and selected articles and illustrations relating to the life and work of Thomas Moran.

EDITED BY

FRITIOF FRYXELL

EAST HAMPTON FREE LIBRARY

EAST HAMPTON, LONG ISLAND,

NEW YORK, 1958

"We live only to discover beauty.
All else is a form of waiting."
Kahlil Gibran

Printed in the United States of America
By the American Book–Stratford Press, Inc., New York, N. Y.

Ruth Bedford Moran. Photograph about 1938.

In memory of

RUTH BEDFORD MORAN

1870–1948

CONTENTS

ILLUSTRATIONS

FOREWORD

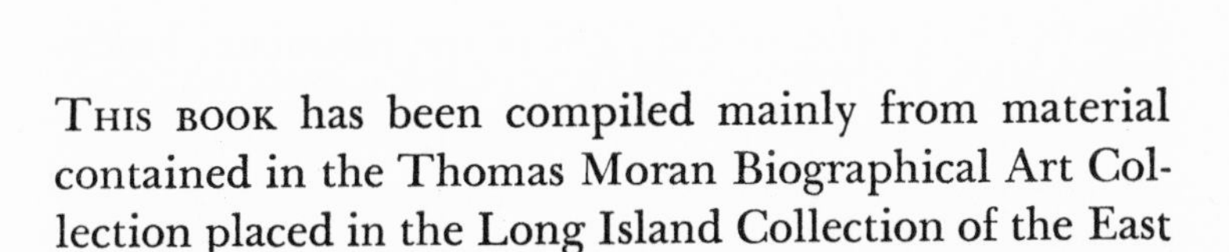

THIS BOOK has been compiled mainly from material contained in the Thomas Moran Biographical Art Collection placed in the Long Island Collection of the East Hampton Free Library by Miss Ruth Bedford Moran as a memorial to her father, Thomas Moran.

For many years Mr. Moran was a resident of this Village, and the numerous sketches and paintings he made of local scenes attest to his fondness and appreciation of the beauty surrounding him. This was his home and final resting place. It seemed natural, therefore, that his daughter should choose our library as custodian of the biographical material which she had assembled. In addition, Miss Moran left a bequest to be used for the care and preservation of this collection, with provisions for its enlargement.

1958 is the tenth anniversary of Miss Moran's death. In her memory and to provide a medium through which information concerning Mr. Moran and his work might become more widely known, this publication was authorized by the Board of Managers.

The library was fortunate in securing as editor Dr.

F. M. Fryxell, who is an accepted authority on Mr. Moran's life and works and a family friend for many years.

The Board of Managers of the East Hampton Free Library acknowledge the assistance given to Mr. Fryxell in his work by Mrs. Robert M. Cheney and Mrs. Amy O. Bassford, of the library staff, by Mrs. Jeannette E. Rattray, of the East Hampton Star, and by Mr. William A. Lockwood, Chairman of the Advisory Board. They also appreciate permission to quote from "Sand and Foam" by Kahlil Gibran, published by Knopf, and to reprint "A Moran Centenary" by Frank Weitenkampf, from the Bulletin of the New York Public Library, and "With Moran in the Yellowstone" by William Henry Jackson, from Appalachia.

JEAN EDWARDS DAYTON, *President*
The Board of Managers,
East Hampton Free Library

THOMAS MORAN

EXPLORER IN SEARCH OF BEAUTY

THOMAS MORAN,

EXPLORER

IN SEARCH OF BEAUTY

FRITIOF FRYXELL

I. THE MAN *

THOMAS MORAN was born in Bolton, Lancashire, England, on January 12, 1837, of Irish-English extraction. His parents, Thomas and Mary Higson Moran, have been described as an "able and artistic" couple. They and their ancestors had been handloom weavers, living in and about Lancashire, and, as one writer put it, "the children of each generation grew up

* This biographical sketch is based on a number of sources, particularly the manuscript and published materials in the Thomas Moran Biographical Art Collection at the East Hampton Free Library, New York, articles I have previously written about Thomas

in the factories, with lives woven in and out with the woof of the week's work."

In 1844 the Moran family immigrated to America. Thus the boy, Thomas, was but seven years of age when he came to this country. The father had visited the New World about a year earlier, to prepare a home, and then had returned to England for his wife and the seven children, Edward, Elizabeth, John, Thomas, Peter, Mary, and Sarah. The family came first to Maryland, but then settled in Philadelphia, where there were better opportunities for the education of the children.

The Morans have been compared to those families "of Flanders three centuries ago or of Japan . . . who seem to have the tendency toward art in the name." While more than a dozen members of this remarkable family achieved eminence in the field of art in America, three brothers from the original family which came here in 1844 stand out first: Edward Moran (1829-1901), the painter of marines and historical scenes; Thomas Moran (1837-1926), the subject of this sketch, best known for his landscape paintings; and Peter Moran (1842-1914), an animal painter and etcher. A

Moran, and the notes which I made during conversations with Mary Moran Tassin and, especially, Ruth B. Moran, the two daughters of the artist, in the course of our long acquaintance. The notes were, as nearly as I could make them, the verbatim records of the information given me.

In using these materials I have tried to correct certain errors in the literature relating to the Morans. As is usually the case, such errors, once published, have been accepted without question by later writers, and thus, through repetition, have come to be widely circulated and well established. F.F.

fourth brother, John Moran (1831-1903), was one of the first and most noted American out-door photographers, and was also a landscape painter. Of the Morans of later generations who became artists, the two sons of Edward, Percy (1862-1935) and Léon (1863-1941) are most widely known.*

Thomas Moran had his education in the public schools of Philadelphia, a cultural and art loving city. He very early manifested intense interest in art and marked aptitude for it. As he studied geography at school, for instance, he made his maps things of beauty and interest, drawing on the margins pictures of Dutchmen, Chinese, or Indians, as the subject might require. And instead of indicating water in the conventional manner, by means of long, waving parallel lines, he made careful pencilings which realistically depicted the waves which had fascinated him on the voyage to America, and he added sketches of ships at sea. He haunted the art stores where the works of various artists, especially those of Philadelphia, were hung, studying the pictures until he learned to know the style and technique of each exhibitor, and could identify the artists represented without looking in the catalogues. Thus he became familiar with the work

* Stephen J. Ferris, husband of Thomas Moran's sister, Elizabeth, was a leading painter and etcher of Philadelphia, as was also their son, J. L. Gerome Ferris. In 1927, J. L. Gerome Ferris presented to the National Gallery of Art (which in 1937 was renamed the National Collection of Fine Arts) of the Smithsonian Institution, at Washington, his father's collection of more than 2300 prints, drawings, etchings, and other pictures. This collection contains many examples of the work of the various Morans, including Thomas and Mary Nimmo Moran.

of such men as Isaac L. Williams, James Hamilton, Washington Allston, Rembrandt Peale, John Neagle, Thomas N. Walter, and John Sartain.

His formal schooling ended when he was fifteen years of age. Having decided to become an artist, but faced also with the necessity of making a living, he became apprenticed to the firm of Scattergood and Telfer, wood engravers, when he was sixteen. He quickly learned to engrave, and his earliest wood engravings are dated 1853, the first year of his apprenticeship. However, he became so skillful at drawing on the blocks of boxwood that drawing, rather than engraving, came to be his usual assignment, a work which gave him the surety of touch that never failed him later in his painting and other work. Meanwhile, he also made many small water color drawings, which the firm took from him and sold. Although his indenture was for a period of seven years, he did not complete his apprenticeship, but left the firm after about three years, when he became seriously ill of a fever.

Upon his recovery, Thomas Moran went to work in a studio which he and his brother, Edward, set up together in Philadelphia. The older, established artists of the city gave him much encouragement, particularly the painter of marines, James Hamilton, to whom he brought his pictures for criticism. This aid Thomas Moran always gratefully acknowledged in later years; however, he never studied with Hamilton or with any other artist, being essentially self-taught.

Hamilton introduced Thomas Moran to the works of the outstanding American and European artists, particularly those of the great English landscape painter, J. M. W. Turner. The young man traded pictures that he had made to an old bookseller, and thus acquired a small but good library of books on art. His book collection included *The Rivers of France, Liber Studiorum,* and other works containing illustrations by Turner. After study of Turner's work, in black-and-white, he eagerly aspired to see his original paintings, in color.

Thomas Moran's first important oil painting, "Among the Ruins There He Lingered," was inspired by Shelley's Alastor. It was painted in 1856, when he was nineteen, and was exhibited in the Pennsylvania Academy of the Fine Arts in 1858. In 1856 and 1857 he made his initial ventures at etching, and in 1860 he made his first lithograph, a marine.

In 1861, Thomas Moran was able to realize his dream of travel abroad, going to London mainly for the purpose of studying, first hand, the paintings of Turner and Claude Lorrain in the galleries of that city. These artists impressed him so deeply that their influence is evident in much of his later work. To learn Turner's technical processes, he carefully copied two or three of his oils, and a larger number of his water colors. When the directors of the National Gallery saw what exquisite work he was doing, they gave him a small empty room where he could work undisturbed, and had pictures brought to him, even some packed away in the basement.*

* Many years later, Moran put his skill in copying Turner to novel use by making one of a series of humorous pictures hung on

After his return to America, in 1862 Thomas Moran was married to Miss Mary Nimmo, daughter of Archibald and Mary Nimmo, of Crescentville, Pennsylvania, a suburb of Philadelphia in which the Morans also had resided. The marriage was the culmination of a long-standing romance. It was not until after her marriage that Mrs. Moran took up art, but her talent was such that, under the tutelage of her husband, she, too, attained eminence, particularly as an etcher. In 1867 the Morans went to England and the Continent for an extended sojourn to study the old Masters. Thomas Moran was little affected by the French art of the day, but responded sympathetically to the romantic feeling and beauty and warmth of color he found in Italian art. On their return to Philadelphia, the Morans entered actively into the artistic life of the city. By 1870 Thomas Moran was an artist of more than local reputation, he was a member of the Pennsylvania Academy of the Fine Arts, and he had exhibited in the Salon in Paris, and elsewhere.

Thomas Moran was never a realist, and was always seeking an outlet for his highly sensitive imagination. He had traveled widely throughout the eastern countryside, and as early as 1860 he had briefly visited the

---

the walls of the parlor of the Salmagundi Club, in New York City, for a special reception given on January 17, 1890, in honor of Ned Abbey, a member recently returned from a long stay abroad. Moran's contribution was a cleverly painted imitation of Turner, done in oil on a round panel. It bore the inscription, "Bought by an American millionaire from a needy English Duke for $291,000.75. Painted by Jim Jam M. W. Turner." *(The Salmagundi Club, A History,* by William Henry Shelton. Cambridge, 1918. Page 56.)

wild Lake Superior country in northern Michigan. It was not until 1871, when he was thirty-four years old, that he made the first of the notable journeys into the Far West that were to establish him as a great, imaginative artist, and the foremost interpreter of western landscapes.

The 1871 expedition was made as guest artist with the Geological Survey of the Territories, under Dr. F. V. Hayden, into the fabulous and still almost unknown Yellowstone region. The impact of this trip on Thomas Moran has been thus expressed by his daughter, Ruth: "Every artist of genius experiences during his life a great spiritual revelation and upheaval. This revelation came to Thomas Moran as he journeyed on horseback through an almost unbelievable wilderness. To him it was all grandeur, beauty, color and light—nothing of man at all, but nature, virgin, unspoiled and lovely. In the Yellowstone country he found fairy-like color and form that his dreams could not rival."

Moran's Yellowstone water colors express the "first ecstasy" of his reaction to these scenes. Another result was the notable oil painting, "Grand Canyon of the Yellowstone," which was recognized as being of such national significance that Congress appropriated ten thousand dollars for its purchase (at the time considered a very large sum), and arranged for its hanging in the Capitol at Washington. This sale made it possible for Thomas Moran to purchase his first studio-home, at Newark, New Jersey; and from now on his reputation and success were assured.

In 1872 Thomas Moran returned to the West, visiting, among other scenic areas, the Yosemite Valley, California. In 1873 his extensive travels included a trip with Major John Wesley Powell, of the United States Geographical and Geological Survey of the Rocky Mountain Region, through the colorful mountains and plateaus of Utah to the north rim of the Grand Canyon of the Colorado River. His first great painting of that subject, "Chasm of the Colorado," was likewise purchased by the Government for ten thousand dollars, and was hung in the Capitol as a companion piece to the Yellowstone painting. In 1874, again with a Hayden Survey party, he penetrated the wilderness of central Colorado, to sketch the mystical Mountain of the Holy Cross. This provided inspiration for what became, probably, the most famous painting ever made of an American mountain. It was awarded the gold medal and diploma of the Centennial Exposition of 1876, at Philadelphia; eventually it was purchased for an English estate, where it still hangs. In the summer of 1874 he also revisited Yosemite, accompanied by his wife, who then had opportunity to see the Far West for the first and, it proved, the only time. In 1879 he and his younger brother, Peter, journeyed with a military escort to the Teton Mountains in Wyoming, which he termed, in his diary, "the finest pictorial range in the United States." Here he sketched, among other subjects, the peak which Dr. Hayden had named "Mount Moran" in his honor a few years earlier.

Companions of the Territorial Surveys called him

"T. Yellowstone Moran," and in the story of the National Parks, Thomas Moran came to hold a unique and honorable place because of the influence he exerted, through his pictures, in bringing the American people to an awareness of their heritage, a country unrivaled in majesty and beauty, with marvelous deserts, mountains, lakes, and forests. The American scene he made his own, and he brought back with him from the Far West a new motif for American artists. He painted the landscapes of a number of National Parks and Monuments, and, by means of his pictures, made them familiar to the public, in each case before they were made into federal sanctuaries. With these areas his name is inseparably linked, especially with Yellowstone, Yosemite, Zion, Grand Canyon, and Grand Teton National Parks.

The strenuous but tremendously fruitful journeys of the '70's were the earliest of a great many that Thomas Moran made, not only to the West but to foreign lands. Even at fourscore years of age, and well beyond, he was still busily recording his impressions of the landscapes whose features his uncanny memory never forgot, the beauty of which never ceased to thrill him. Though always he considered himself to be primarily a painter of the American scene, his range of subjects was exceptionally large, covering, besides the varied aspects of his adopted land, those of other countries he visited and revisited, especially England and Italy; also many pictures purely of the imagination.

Throughout Thomas Moran's long life he was extraordinarily productive. Early in his career he illustrated books and magazines, his work in this field ranking with the best and being in great demand. His production has been estimated at well over 1500 illustrations, of which number about two-thirds were woodcuts. He made illustrations for Scribner's Monthly Magazine, The Aldine Magazine of Art, and other current periodicals; for the reports of the Hayden and Powell Surveys; for school texts; for travel books, such as *Picturesque America, The Overland Tourist,* and *Picturesque California;* for special editions of the poetry of Longfellow, Whittier, Lloyd Mifflin and others.

The great folio volume by Dr. F. V. Hayden, *Yellowstone National Park, and the Mountain Regions of Portions of Idaho, Nevada, Colorado, and Utah,* published by Louis Prang at Boston in 1876, contains fifteen chromolithographic reproductions of water colors by Thomas Moran. This volume has been termed "unexcelled among books on the Far West for the astonishing magnificence of its plates, which have never been surpassed either in importance or beauty . . . These are the illustrations which first adequately revealed to the world the extraordinary scenes they depict, and by common consent they have since held supreme rank." (Catalogue of the Holiday collection of Western Americana, New York, 1954.)

Thomas Moran made many lithographs in addition to those prepared as illustrations; and he also worked with charcoal. He was in the front rank of American etchers, most of his many etchings being made during the decade from 1878 to 1888. John Ruskin, the

English art critic and author, who became his friend and correspondent and who purchased some of his pictures, characterized his etching, "The Wave, East Hampton," as the finest line-drawn etching of moving water he had ever seen.

Thomas Moran was equally well known for his water colors and oils. Of the hundreds of pictures he painted, a few may be mentioned to suggest the nature of his themes: Children of the Mountains; A Dream of the Orient; Solitude; Shoshone Falls, Idaho; The Rock Towers of the Colorado; The Pearl of Venice; The Glory of the Canyon; A Dream City; On the Bright Angel Trail; Flight into Egypt; Summit of the Sierras; Hiawatha and the Serpents; Passing Shower in the Yellowstone Canyon; Coast of Newfoundland; Fingal's Cave, Scotland; Castle at Green River, Wyoming; The Sunny Glade; A Day in Old Mexico; Spectres from the North—Icebergs in Mid-Atlantic; Grand Canyon of Arizona, Pillar of Cloud and Fire; Arabian Nights; Venetian Festival; A Tower of Cortez, Mexico; An Iowa Gulch; Sunset, East Hampton; The Lotus Eaters; After the Rain; The Palace and the Prison; Church Door, Moravatio; The Smelters, Denver; A Lancashire Village; Twilight; The Rescuing Party; "Childe Roland to the dark tower came"; The Newark Meadows; A Sand Storm at Acoma, New Mexico; The Solitary Horseman; Sunset, the Pacific; Fiesta, Mexico; Mid-Ocean, Moonlight.

The many awards for his pictures include the medals of the Centennial Exposition of 1876, Philadelphia; the Columbian Exposition of 1893, Chicago; the Pan-

American Exposition of 1901, St. Louis; and the American Art Association of Philadelphia, 1902.

He was a member of The National Academy of Design, The Art Club of Philadelphia, The American Water Color Society, The New York Etching Club, The Royal Society of Painter-Etchers, London, and the Painters of the West (Honorary). He also was a member of the Salmagundi Club (serving as the fourth president of the club, from 1893 to 1896), The Century Club, The Tile Club, and The Lotos Club of New York.

Moran's studios were successively located in Philadelphia, Newark, New York City, and, finally, in the quaint old village of East Hampton at the eastern end of Long Island. From 1879 on, the Morans regarded East Hampton as their home. They resided there the greater part of each year, in the spacious Studio which Thomas Moran built in 1884, "surrounded by the quiet restfulness of old windmills, orchards and green fields, with the broad Atlantic almost at his door." Here most of Thomas Moran's important work was done.

Thomas Moran loved all beautiful things, good music, and great books. (Among his favorites were The Arabian Nights, Aesops Fables, Don Quixote, Young's Night Thoughts, and the poems of Robert Browning.) In the Studio he surrounded himself with objets d'art from many lands, the treasures gathered on his travels. He maintained this Studio for more than forty years, to the end of his life; his daughter, Ruth, preserved it unchanged more than two decades longer, until her own death.

Thomas Moran's wife died in 1899; his son, Paul Nimmo Moran, a genre painter, died in 1907. His two daughters, Mary Moran Tassin and Ruth Bedford Moran, survived him, the former until 1955, the latter until 1948. He himself lived to become the senior member of the National Academy of Design and revered as the Dean of American Artists, dying in Santa Barbara, California, on August 25, 1926, at the age of 89.

Ruth Moran has given this account of her father's last days. "He died looking at the cracks of the ceiling, making Venice out of their patterns, just as, all his life, he had lingered at marble panels and stained wood, seeing pictures in the lines. On his death-bed he insisted that we leave a closet door wide open. We protested that it should be shut, but still he wanted it left open. Finally we understood why; when the door was closed it threw a shadow over the ceiling cracks. In those last hours he was thinking not of daughter, friends, or death, but of pictures."

In a catalogue printed for one of the memorial exhibitions held in a New York art gallery, in observance of the Centenary of Thomas Moran, appears this statement:

"He passed his own way uninfluenced by fads and upheavals in Art. . . . He lived a long and happy life in Art, for to him Art was Life itself. Wrapped in the mantle of his own aloofness, he had the independence dear to genius. He was a lover of nature and a lover of solitude. His art today stands alone, belonging to no school, but is Thomas Moran. A prophet of the Old Testament wrote these lines, 'your old men shall dream dreams, your young men shall see visions.' It came true in Thomas Moran. Seeing, he dreamed and painted his visioning."

The works of Thomas Moran may be found in many art galleries and other institutions. Important collections of his pictures are at the East Hampton Free Library, Long Island, New York; Cooper Union Art Center, New York City; New York Public Library; National Collection of Fine Arts of the Smithsonian Institution, Washington, D. C.; the Gilcrease Institute of American History and Art, and the Philbrook Art Center, both at Tulsa, Oklahoma; Yellowstone and Grand Teton National Parks, Wyoming; Yosemite National Park, California; Sheffield Museum and Chiswick Museum, England.

In the beautiful Guild Hall at East Hampton, New York, is an art gallery named in honor of Thomas Moran. On the brink of three great canyons in the West—the Grand Canyon of the Yellowstone, in Wyoming; Yosemite Valley, in California; and the Grand Canyon of the Colorado, in Arizona—are promontories which bear the name, "Moran Point," reminiscent of the fact that these were favorite vantages from which, many years ago, he made his studies. Not far south of Yellowstone, in Grand Teton National Park, are Moran Canyon and Mount Moran. Mount Moran, giant of the Tetons, is the most monumental peak in this range, a mountain almost unrivaled as regards grandeur of form and beauty of setting. The features of few mountains have become as familiar to the American public as have those of Mount Moran, and probably no mountain in this country is now more often photographed and painted. It is a fitting memorial to Thomas Moran, the artist-explorer whose journeys were made in search of beauty.

II. STORY OF THE THOMAS MORAN COLLECTION AT EAST HAMPTON

The cliché which holds that "what a man achieves is the measure of some woman's influence" might be applied to Thomas Moran, except that, in his case, it would seem that three dedicated women made possible his great career: his mother, his wife, and his younger daughter.

Of his mother, Mary Higson Moran, less is known than one could wish, although there is, of course, that record which any true mother would put first, the good repute of her children. She must have been a very exceptional woman. It could not have been otherwise, for—as the mother in the household which she and her husband established in Philadelphia, after their transplanting from English soil—she helped create a cultural environment which caused each one of the many children in this poor immigrant's family to seek artistic expression. And when the children one after the other found art irresistible, in choosing a life's work, the mother (and the father, too, it should be added) gave them warm encouragement. The boy, Thomas, was among these. At sixteen he embarked on a career in art, he met with success, and while still a relatively young man he became renowned as one of the leading artists of America. Immeasurable but great must have been the influence of this mother on her child, the "father of the man."

As Thomas Moran thus became absorbed in art, and art in turn absorbed him, he manifested some of the personal traits reputed to be not uncommon among those of pronounced artistic temperament. His daughter, Ruth, said of him, "From the beginning to the end of his long life, my father was a dreamer and a painter of dreams. He would forget everything except his painting." Again, "He had not the capacity for looking far ahead, and seeing and planning for the future. Hence others always planned for him."

Accordingly, his marriage to the bonnie Scottish lass, Mary Nimmo, also an immigrant, was a particularly fortunate one, for in addition to being charming and lovable she was, in her daughter's words, "canny, farseeing, and frugal." She was all this, and more; she was talented, and wise. Thomas and Mary Nimmo Moran were completely devoted to each other; but living always in and for his art, Thomas Moran would sometimes prove forgetful and take many things somewhat for granted, even his wife and the children. To meet this situation, Mary Nimmo Moran herself quickly took up art and studied it from her husband, in order better to make a place for herself in his life, and to give him every opportunity to realize his great possibilities. Despite the cares of home, husband, and three children, she achieved high recognition in her own right; nevertheless this was, from her point of view, quite incidental. "Without mother," recalled Ruth Moran, "father could never have become what he did. She never allowed any barrier to come between him and his destiny—which was to paint ceaselessly."

In the fall of 1899, when she was only 57, death claimed Mary Nimmo Moran. Soldiers returned from Cuba and hospitalized at Camp Wikoff, on Montauk Point, Long Island, brought in typhoid, which spread to nearby East Hampton, home of the Morans. Ruth caught the disease, and in nursing her, Mrs. Moran herself contracted it. Told that her daughter could not live, the mother was unable to hold up longer, was put to bed, and two weeks later, on September 25, succumbed. Ruth did recover, and giving up her career as a Shakespearean reader, thereafter lived with no other thought than to take her mother's place and try to do for Thomas Moran what Mary Nimmo had done.

Knowing that unless her father could forget his grief in work he could not again accomplish much, before she was yet strong Ruth took him on a long tour of the West—to Yellowstone, the Colorado Rockies, the Grand Canyon, and other scenic areas known to him from his early journeys and replete with happy memories. This was the first of many trips that they two, father and daughter, made together, for from then on, whither Thomas Moran went Ruth went too.

Illness having depleted their savings, Ruth Moran became, in her words, "business manager" for the two of them. Like her mother she proved competent, assuming responsibility for their joint housekeeping, wherever that might be, and also for travel arrangements, exhibitions, picture sales, and correspondence. (Letters by Thomas Moran, dated after 1900, are virtually non-existent, because his daughter did practically all his writing for him.) So Ruth's place in the life of her father did become much like that of Mary Nimmo's; with reference to it their intimate California friend, Charles Lummis, once termed her "daughter, sister, mother, and chum." As the years slipped by, peacefully for the most part, and patriarchal old age came to Thomas Moran, he and Ruth finally, in 1916, left the Studio at East Hampton and repaired to Santa Barbara, California. They still made frequent pilgrimages to the Grand Canyon, Yosemite, and other favorite places, and he continued to paint as late as 1924. It was at Santa Barbara that he died, in 1926.

Ruth Moran survived her father by twenty-two years. During this period she maintained the Studio at East Hampton as it had been in her father's life, residing there most of the time except for the winter months, which she generally spent in New York City. The life and work of Thomas Moran continued to be her absorbing interest, and to it she gave all that her strength would permit. That she accomplished so much, even through years of poor health, was a source of wonder and inspiration to her friends.

There was endless correspondence to answer: inquiries concerning Thomas Moran's life and, particularly, his paintings, now scattered by the hundreds through this country and abroad, and frequently listed

Mary Higson Moran, mother of the artist. Etching by J. L. Gerome Ferris, a grandson. 1879.

Thomas Moran, Senior, father of the artist.

Thomas Moran's artist brothers: Edward, John, Peter.

Thomas Moran, at about the age of 16 years.

Illustration for "An Island of the Sea"
Scribner's Magazine September 1878.

Thomas Moran, in 1921, at the age of 84. Photo by Gledhill.

Thomas Moran, in 1926, at the age of 89. Photo by Gledhill.

Mary Nimmo, as a young woman. From a daguerreotype.

The Moran family. Silhouettes made about the time the Morans moved to East Hampton. Thomas Moran and his wife, Mary Nimmo Moran; their son, Paul Nimmo Moran; and their daughters, Mary Scott Moran and Ruth Bedford Moran.

Thomas Moran at work, etching, in his New York Studio. 1885.

The Studio, East Hampton, Long Island, about 1900. Thomas Moran standing by fence.

Interior of the Studio, East Hampton, about 1900 (much as it appeared throughout a period of more than sixty years).

Wood engraving by Thomas Moran. Inscribed by him, "The Catawissa Valley, one of my earliest drawings on wood. T. Moran. 1853."

Lithograph by Thomas Moran. Inscribed by him, "My First Lithograph. 1860."

Green River, Wyoming. 1871. One of Thomas Moran's first sketches in the West.

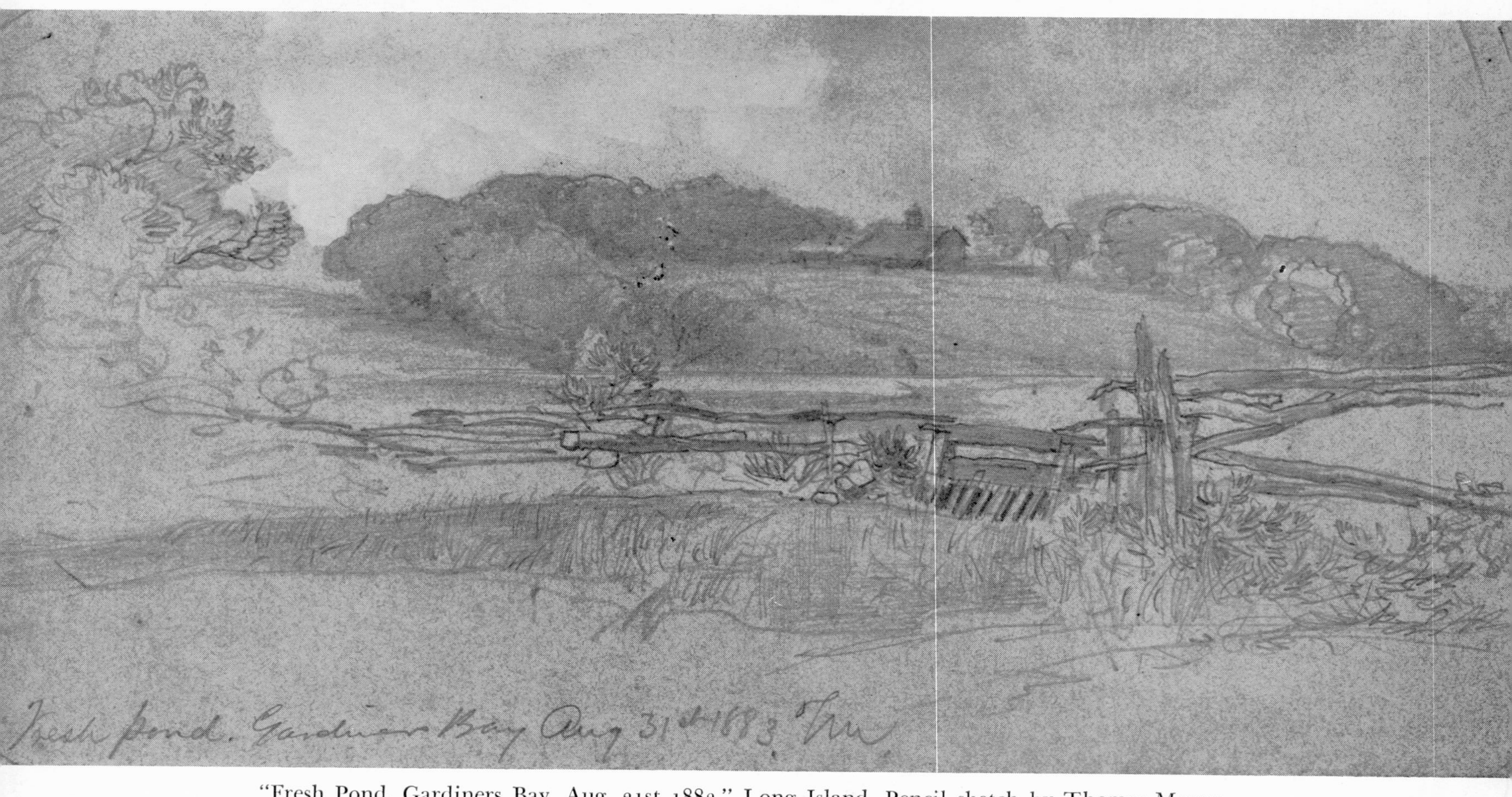

"Fresh Pond. Gardiners Bay. Aug. 31st 1883." Long Island. Pencil sketch by Thomas Moran.

by art dealers; queries concerning places, subjects, dates, and signatures (for not infrequently imitations appeared on the market). Her aid was solicited, as a matter of course, in connection with art exhibits devoted to, or including, the works of Thomas and Mary Nimmo Moran. For these occasions often she not only furnished needed information but also loaned pictures of her own from the Studio, or arranged for loans by others, so that the displays might have proper balance. The task of selecting, framing, crating, and shipping the pictures was in many instances a huge one, especially during the years 1936 and 1937, when exhibitions observing the Centenary of Thomas Moran were held from coast to coast. Whenever possible she attended the exhibitions in person; often she aided with the arranging and hanging of the pictures.

Ruth Moran was also much concerned with the problem of providing for the hundreds of original sketches left by her father, and the reference materials relating to his work which she had retained for her own use or kept simply to enjoy as long as she could. With respect to this problem, Thomas Moran had himself made a beginning by presenting a set of his works (nearly one hundred examples illustrating everything from the slightest pencil sketches to finished pictures of various kinds) to the Cooper Union Art Center in New York City,—an institution he enthusiastically supported, and in which he had great faith, because of the encouragement and aid it gave to needy art students.

Following her father's example, therefore, Ruth

Moran from time to time distributed pictures among several existing collections,—especially lithographs, and etchings by Thomas and Mary Nimmo Moran; she gave assistance, whenever possible, to art galleries and various institutions endeavoring to acquire the works of her parents; and in the course of years she herself established several new collections, notably the following:

In 1930 she made a selection of sketches, water colors, and other items relating to the Teton Mountains in Wyoming, and presented these to the Grand Teton National Park, which had been created by act of Congress the year previous. Items from this collection have been on exhibition since that year, at the park museum, situated not far from the base of Mount Moran. The new and improved museum facilities now being provided in this park should soon permit exhibition of this collection under highly favorable conditions.

On October 1, 1935, Ruth Moran presented to the National Park Service a much larger collection, numbering nearly three hundred items relating to various western National Parks and Monuments. When fully prepared this splendid collection, "The Thomas Moran Collection of the National Parks," was placed on display, in large part, at the museum in Yosemite National Park, in August, 1936, at which time Miss Moran made the trip to California in order to assist with the arrangements.* The exhibition at Yosemite was continued through 1937 in observance of the

* Yosemite Nature Notes, Thomas Moran Number, Volume XV, Number 8 (August, 1936).

Thomas Moran Centenary, after which most of it had to go into storage. As new and larger museums are built in the National Parks this collection will undoubtedly again be displayed. It was Miss Moran's hope that the collection might eventually go to Yellowstone, because of the deep attachment which she and her father had for that park, and because there it could be exhibited together with the superb series of Thomas Moran water colors of the Yellowstone presented to the nation in 1927 as a joint gift from George D. Pratt, John D. Rockefeller, Jr., Colonel Herbert J. Slocum, and Mrs. Henry Strong.**

In the summer of 1935 Miss Moran also assembled another collection, to which she had long given serious thought, "The Thomas Moran Biographical Art Collection." She chose this name for the collection because in it she included reference material of biographical and like significance; to this, however, she added many representative etchings, lithographs, sketches, and additional items, particularly such as related to East Hampton and vicinity. Her wish was to have this collection given a permanent home, after her death, in

** In a letter dated September 16, 1958, Mr. Lemuel A. Garrison, Superintendent of Yellowstone National Park, informed the editor that the collection at Yellowstone includes "22 original Moran field sketches made in the Yellowstone in 1871 and 1892." Fourteen of the sketches are at present stored in the safe of the Mammoth Museum; eight are on display in the visitor center at the new Canyon Village. Yellowstone Park also has "an oil painting which the Yellowstone Library and Museum Association purchased from Haynes Studios, Inc., and then presented as a gift to the National Park Service. This painting is now on display in the visitor center at Canyon Village."

the East Hampton Free Library, which she regarded as the logical repository for this material in view of the long residence of the Morans in East Hampton, her own deep interest in the library, and the splendid facilities there available, including fireproof housing. To her proposal, Mrs. Ettie Hedges Pennypacker, Librarian, and her husband, the late Morton Pennypacker, donor of the Library's Long Island Collection, gave hearty approval. In drafting her will, Miss Moran made generous provision for the future upkeep of the Collection.

During the winter of 1947-1948, Ruth Moran, though now past 77 years of age and in precarious health, revisited her friends at Santa Barbara, California. There, in the spring, she became critically ill, and she died on May 10, the date on which she was to have begun her return trip to New York. Her ashes were interred at East Hampton, in the family lot in the old South End Burying Ground, by her parents and brother. In accordance with the terms of her will, the material designated as "The Thomas Moran Biographical Art Collection" was transferred from the Studio to the East Hampton Free Library—a move of only a few hundred yards—and placed in the Gertrude Mumford Memorial Room. Here the collection has been given every care, is now being catalogued and otherwise prepared for use, and is being augmented, from time to time, as gifts are received and items purchased for it.

It should be added that, at the time of Ruth Moran's death, there still remained in her possession much unassigned material. Fortunately, in the final disposition of the estate, the most important part of this residue was kept intact, and was acquired by the Gilcrease Institute of American History and Art, at Tulsa, Oklahoma. Addition of this material—hundreds of sketches and other original works *—to the numerous oil paintings and other pictures by Thomas Moran at the Gilcrease Institute, and also at the nearby Philbrook Art Center, gives Tulsa a body of material, representing the work of this artist, which is unique in quality and comprehensiveness.

The tenth anniversary of the death of Ruth Moran has provided the occasion for issuing this publication. It has been prepared with a view to making the collection at the East Hampton Free Library more widely known, by indicating the nature and scope of its contents, particularly for the benefit of those who may wish to consult the resources which it now makes available.

---

* In a letter dated September 5, 1958, Mr. James T. Forrest, Executive Director of the Thomas Gilcrease Institute, made the following statement to the editor: "In all, we have over 600 sketches, more than 100 water colors and 27 oils (by Thomas Moran). We also have a painting of Moran by William Merritt Chase . . . the Philbrook Art Center has 3 or 4 oils by Moran. We have had special exhibits of Moran's paintings and consider our collection of this famous American landscape artist as one of the finest segments of our extensive collection . . . our collection also contains several photographs, proof copies of lithographs and etchings done by Moran and several personal papers."

III. THE COLLECTION

As has been noted, the Thomas Moran Collection at the East Hampton Free Library is one of several relating to the work of this artist. Of the various collections scattered about the country, each has its own distinctive character and significance. The East Hampton collection, as compared with the others, is one of the more important, and in certain respects it is quite unique for it contains material which, by its very nature, cannot be fully duplicated elsewhere.

Ruth Moran intended that this collection should be the main depository for material of a biographical nature pertaining to her parents; this it now is, and it should become increasingly important for reference purposes as it is further developed. Even now, any research relating to the life and work of these artists would be incomplete, and also to some extent inaccurate, were it to neglect the sources of information in the East Hampton collection. Further, the collection contains important data concerning the brothers of Thomas Moran and the other artists of the family.

Manuscript materials as such are relatively limited in the collection, at least as compared with some of the other categories of material. This is due, in part, to the fact that Thomas Moran himself was too absorbed in the actual work of painting to have either time or inclination for writing, being content to let his creative work stand as the record of his career. There are some items from the hand of Thomas Moran—mostly records of pictures and sales—and a single item written by Mary Nimmo Moran, an incomplete autobiographical note on one sheet of paper; the rest is mainly material written by Ruth Moran or prepared by others who collaborated with her.

Miss Moran at times hoped it would be possible for her to write a definitive biography of her father. That she never accomplished this writing is to be regretted deeply, for no-one knew the facts of his career, or understood his purposes and work, as well as she. However, the incessant demands on her time and strength for secretarial and other duties, together with uncertain health, prevented her from ever carrying out this plan. She did, however, give aid whenever possible to others who were interested in writing about her distinguished parents. Many short biographical accounts and studies of the work of Thomas and Mary Nimmo Moran were written, often with her assistance, and these were published in various reference volumes, art journals, and elsewhere. The collection at East Hampton contains about fifty published articles of this nature, and some of the copies on file are especially valuable because of marginal corrections and other notations inserted by Miss Moran.

On several occasions Miss Moran furnished information to persons who undertook to write more comprehensively about Thomas Moran. However, no biography or other study of book size was ever carried through to completion. Some chapters which were written, in rough draft, are preserved in the collection, and since Miss Moran took care to save them it may be assumed that they have a certain amount of reference value if used critically.

The collection also contains much correspondence—most of it Miss Moran's—only a small part of which has thus far been sorted and arranged.

A notable feature of the collection is the large number of original sketches by Thomas Moran which it contains,—more than two hundred in all. These are mostly pencil sketches, but there are many black-and-white wash drawings, and some water colors and pen-and-ink sketches. Among the sketches are many which have great local interest because they depict Long Island subjects, especially scenes in and around East Hampton. However, their significance is far more than local. Many consulting this collection will find these sketches to be the most interesting items in it, since they are, as has often been pointed out, Thomas Moran's "notes," the records of his on-the-spot impressions. These impressions his memory retained to an extraordinary degree; however, at times he did use the sketches themselves for reference purposes, as he painted the "finished" oil paintings and water colors in the Studio. Artists today find in these original sketches an artistry and spontaneity which make them in many ways even more appealing than the pictures based on them. Thomas Moran's original sketches have become widely scattered, and the series in the East Hampton collection form an important group, complementing those in the other collections which have been mentioned. It was Miss Moran's wish that a considerable number of sketches of Long Island subjects should remain at East Hampton, and so, fittingly, they have.

Another important part of the collection is its extensive series of illustrations by Thomas Moran. Most of these are woodcuts, but there are examples of other types as well. The work of illustrating was largely confined to Thomas Moran's earlier years, from 1853 to about 1883; the relatively little illustrating which he did in later years was mainly for personal friends, like the poets, Henry N. Dodge and Lloyd Mifflin. During the Philadelphia and Newark periods of his career, making illustrations was his principal means of livelihood, as it brought him a definite and dependable income, whereas the sale of paintings was more unpredictable. In order to have his days and the advantages of daylight for painting, he did most of his illustrating at night, since the work in black-and-white it involved could be done by the imperfect gas light. In the case of the woodcuts, Thomas Moran generally made the drawings on the blocks of boxwood, and the actual work of engraving these by hand (a now all but forgotten art) was then done by others. In the East Hampton collection are more than 500 of Thomas Moran's illustrations, an unequalled selection representative of this phase of the artist's work. A large proportion of these are proofs, printed on special paper. The collection of illustrations also includes twelve of the famous Prang chromolithographs made in 1876 from water colors by Thomas Moran.

In the East Hampton collection are more than 150 examples of the curious creations by Thomas Moran which he called his "metamorphoses." He began making these during the winter following his wife's death, for his own relaxation and to please his children. They were produced in the evenings, at the boarding house in New York where the family then stayed, following his day's work when he had not time to return to the studio. Having read the newspaper (none too thoroughly) he would throw it on the floor, then study the pictures on the page. Any picture would do, one illustrating a current event, a map, a fashion drawing, or one depicting animals or some person in the news. If at first the picture did not suggest a landscape, he would walk around it until, when he viewed it from a certain angle, new forms were suggested. Presently he would settle down over the paper, with the latter as often sidewise or inverted as right side up; and he would start touching up the outlines of the chosen picture with eraser, pencil, or white water color. Quickly, a transformation would take place. A picture captioned "Inspecting the Fort Arthur Garrison" became a Scene in Venice; another, "Wrecked by a Misplaced Switch," became an Adobe Pueblo of the Southwest; a third, "Mrs. Legrand Benedict," became a Landscape with Trees and Mountains; a fourth, "Henrietta Crossman in 'Sweet Kitty Bellairs,'" became a Scene with Ruined Castle and Bridge. At first he did a thorough job, so that when the change was completed he had produced a finished landscape; but later he touched up his "metamorphoses" more lightly, so that when turned in the right manner the original illustration was clearly discernible. Often he left the original caption, which amusingly gave an incongruous name to the landscape and indicated from what subject it had been evolved. So, many nights, through many years. "I have gotten some good compositions out of the newspapers," he once remarked. Other artists marveled at the beauty of these creations, many of which were comparable to his finished pictures, and urged him to have them photographed because of the perishability of the newspaper stock; but having made them he was heedless and did not look at them again. However, his daughter saved many and mounted them in scrapbooks. The "metamorphoses" fascinate all who see them, and they throw much light on the mind and methods of this artist, who discerned imagery in whatever came before his eyes.

A valuable unit of the collection is a series of more than 300 photographs of pictures painted by Thomas Moran. This is the reference set assembled by Miss Moran through the years as she was called on by art dealers, galleries, and individuals to authenticate pictures painted by her father, and for other information. Most of the photographs bear her annotations on the reverse side, such as the date, title, and owner of each picture. These annotations greatly increase the usefulness of the series.

Only a detailed catalogue of the collection at East Hampton can indicate how many other items of unusual interest and value it contains. There are, for example, many original sketches, etchings, and paintings by members of the Moran family other than Thomas and Mary Nimmo Moran. Represented in this series are Edward Moran, Percy Moran, Léon Moran,

Paul Nimmo Moran, Charles Moran (son of Peter Moran), Stephen J. Ferris (brother-in-law of Thomas Moran), and J. L. Gerome Ferris (son of Stephen J. Ferris); also a number of pictures made by friends of the Morans. There is a splendid series of photographs, both formal and informal, of Thomas Moran; many others of Mary Nimmo Moran; some of their children, close relatives, and friends; a number of their studios. There is a collection of more than one hundred reproductions in color of paintings by Thomas Moran. Mention should be made of a large scrapbook in which are newspaper articles and other items dating as far back as the '70's; several family photo albums; and a bound volume of early landscape photographs by John Moran, now of considerable historic interest. In the collection are a number of personal mementoes such as brushes, tubes of paint, and water colors used by Thomas Moran; three of his palettes; the medals and certificates awarded to Thomas and Mary Nimmo Moran; a family guest book from the Studio; and the beautiful East Indian carved teakwood chest which stood for decades in the Studio. The collection includes the bust of Thomas Moran, in bronze, made by the sculptor, J. S. Hartley, in 1891. (Two copies of this bust are owned by the National Park Service, one being at Yosemite National Park and the other at Grand Teton National Park.)

At present the East Hampton Free Library possesses only one important oil painting by Thomas Moran, "The Owls" (size 30 by 35 inches). Painted in 1917, it was presented to the library by Mrs. Lorenzo E. Woodhouse. There is a fine oil (size 16 by 20 inches) by Mary Nimmo Moran, "In Dr. E. Osborn's Garden, East Hampton," painted in 1895; also an oil portrait (size 16 by 20 inches) by Paul Nimmo Moran of his sister, Mary Moran Tassin, painted in 1895 (the year of her marriage). There is a good selection of etchings by both Thomas Moran and Mary Nimmo Moran, as well as many lithographs and a representative set of steel engravings by Thomas Moran.

The collection contains more than fifty catalogues of sales and exhibitions which included the works of the Morans; also about sixty selected volumes which form an excellent nucleus for a special library devoted to Thomas Moran and the Moran family.

From this summary it should be evident that the collection at East Hampton may be expected to serve a number of purposes, falling, in the main, into two categories:

Research and reference purposes: These uses might include

1. General studies, both brief and more comprehensive, relating to the life and work of Thomas Moran, Mary Nimmo Moran, and other artists of the family;

2. More specialized art studies, such as Thomas Moran's work as an illustrator, his use of the various media of art, and the place of Mary Nimmo Moran among the pioneer women etchers of America;

3. Investigations pertaining to individual pictures by Thomas Moran (for example, the history of certain

pictures, and the detection of "fake pictures" alleged to be the work of Thomas Moran);

4. Compilation of a catalogue of the works of Thomas Moran in the art collections of this country and elsewhere;

5. Studies relating to artists of the West, and the place of Thomas Moran in art movements of his period;

6. Local studies, concerned with events and celebrities of East Hampton and Long Island.

Exhibition purposes: These uses might include

1. Occasional, temporary displays, such as for special occasions, e.g. anniversaries, and exhibitions devoted to artists of East Hampton and Long Island, or to painters of the West;

2. Permanent displays of items from the collection, e.g. original works of Thomas and Mary Nimmo Moran and other artists of the family, and interesting memorabilia.

What has been stated should make it abundantly clear that the Thomas Moran Biographical Art Collection is one of the outstanding treasures among the special collections of the East Hampton Free Library, and it is one that has general as well as local importance. When it becomes better known, both in the immediate community and in the larger circles embracing art galleries, schools, and libraries throughout the country, its significance should be widely recognized, and as it is developed its importance should increase with the years.

One may predict that local students and outside scholars will more and more utilize the Thomas Moran Collection for purposes such as those suggested, and that in time the collection will, to an increasingly great degree, fulfill the purposes for which it was established. And the collection will stand as a perpetual and inspiring reminder of Ruth Moran's lifelong, selfless devotion to her father, as well as her own unswerving loyalty to the ideals for which he stood.

THOMAS MORAN:

AN IMPRESSION

RUTH B. MORAN *

THE FIRST IMPRESSION of my father was—and I believe the last impression will be—the atmosphere of romance that he had about him. He seemed always to be starting off or coming back from strange, beautiful places, wild countries. And then on the return I would be thrilled by the lovely colors that almost at once began to grow and glow on canvas and water-color pads, and the delicate, beautiful drawings on the blocks of boxwood.

I used to come padding down in my nightgown and bare feet, lured by the talk that drifted up the stairs to my crib, and curl up in my mother's lap to be nearer, night after night, as my father sat drawing numberless illustrations for school books and magazines

* From The Mentor, August, 1924.

—all the then new wonders of the "Far West" that so captivated and thrilled him with their beauty and romance.

Thomas Moran's whole figure was romantic, perhaps the more so because of the utter lack of self-consciousness—the eyes not dreamy but clear and far-seeing, shining like a child's eyes. Always they have had, and still have, the look of seeing, and remembering, wonders. His mouth was delicate for a man's, but practically hidden by his beard and moustache of fair hair—his nose was delicate and sensitive. He used always to wear, in winter, a round beaver fur cap, set rather jauntily on his very small, compact head. Nearly five feet seven inches in height, thin, wiry, and quick and firm on his feet, with perfect balance—he wore his cap and cape coat rather gallantly. Yes, he was a romantic figure, in a not very romantic period. He was quick-witted, full of humor, kind and very generous; but quick-tempered, also, and a good fighter for any cause that he might take up.

He loved music, playing the violin by ear only, but playing with spirit; and as I first remember him, always singing with a good, sweet tenor voice. Loving his children, but forgetting them so completely when at work—which was practically always—that I have no recollection of ever asking, or depending on him, for anything.

I do not think he ever reproved me or attempted any kind of discipline in his life; he did not believe in discipline for children, nor the theory of discipline for anyone. His children, three of us, loved him, and never felt the least awe or fear of him, but always instinctively an awe of his work. He, himself, disappeared so completely in it—was so rapt in it—that we children never had to be told, or taught, to reverence it—it was always the first thought of all of us—as it was practically the whole thought and life of my father.

We lived closely as a family, always in and out of the studio, but we never disturbed my father. We would lie flat on the floor and watch him paint, or use his water colors to paint the pictures for ourselves in the old pictorial magazine, "The Aldine"; or we would shudder with delightful horror over the Doré drawings in Dante's "Inferno," which was always in the studio, but we never disturbed the complete concentration which isolated Thomas Moran from everyone he most loved—even his beloved wife, who was almost a part of himself.

He was never at any time really interested in making money, and always was the worst possible salesman for his pictures; almost anyone could get a picture cheapened in price if he would only stay long enough in the studio, for my father was always aching to get back to work, to get to his easel, and get rid of the buyer.

He took a great joy in all beautiful artistic things; rugs, and bronzes—and he spent his money lavishly to get them. Certain things that he and my mother bought in their youth he has taken with him whenever he traveled away from home, because something in their form or beauty was necessary to him, and so appealed that he felt their need wherever he might be.

His concentration on his art, his utter lack of introspection, and his lack of interest in people as a whole, have made him personally and intimately known to very few, but his friendships have been great friendships, full of trust and sincerity and love.

He has always been the most modest of men, but his own great sincerity of nature has given him little patience with the worldly wise or insincere; and all his life he has been ready with lance in rest to fight to the death for any of the principles of the art that he himself has been ready to risk health, happiness, and even life itself, to attain.

So now when I look at him, in his eighty-eighth year, unchanged in spirit, still noting every variation of light and color and form in the clouds, the solidity of the foliage of the live oak, and the grace of the eucalyptus; still dreaming his fairy cities and strange, misty mountain-rimmed seas—I feel again the old thrill and wonder of Romance, as I did in my babyhood when I crept down the stairs and into my mother's lap to watch him at work on his black and white dreams, after a long day with color—never tired, never through, always riding on through his enchanted forest.

A PEN-PICTURE OF

MARY NIMMO MORAN

A. DEMONTAIGUE *

MARY NIMMO MORAN was born in Strathaven, Scotland, in the year 1842. Although a foreigner by nativity, the artist was completely identified with the country of her adoption. She was in every sense an American, and an ardent admirer of the United States, where she scored so many artistic triumphs.

She was married to Mr. Thomas Moran, the well known painter. Dating from the period of her marriage, Mrs. Moran became a devotee of art, studying

---

* From The Art Stationer, July, 1888. About 1900, shortly after the death of Mrs. Moran, her husband and daughter, Ruth, inserted minor corrections and revisions in the margins of a copy of this article, now in the Thomas Moran Collection at East Hampton. As here reprinted, the article incorporates these changes.

For a fuller biographical sketch of Mary Nimmo Moran see the National Cyclopedia of Biography (American), volume 22 (1932), page 25.

with great assiduity, both in oil and water color under the guidance of her husband.

In the year 1867 they both made the tour of Europe, visiting the different picture galleries and making their home in Paris near the Luxembourg Galleries for nine months. They returned with a portfolio of sketches of some of the quaint and romantic corners of the Old World.

In 1871 Mr. and Mrs. Moran removed from Philadelphia to Newark, New Jersey, and later to New York, making a congenial home for themselves in the great art center of the United States.

Although Mrs. Moran's fame as an etcher has quite overshadowed the memory of her achievements as a painter, she, at the outset of her career, exhibited several times in the National Academy of Design, her pictures receiving high encomiums.

In the year 1874, in company with her husband she visited the western states. In 1879, Mr. Moran contemplating another tour in that region of the country, his wife decided to remain at home, she with her three children going to Easton, Pennsylvania. Before his departure, Mr. Moran coated several copper plates, advising his wife to employ her leisure moments in etching them. These first attempts were necessarily experimental, as Mrs. Moran possessed but scant knowledge of the art of etching, and her husband being absent, she was unassisted by his advice and experience. The work was done for the purpose of recreation and with but little expectation of being successful. When on her husband's return she showed him the result of her labors, he found the methods so entirely original that he scarcely knew whether to pronounce it a success or failure. With many misgivings, four of the plates were submitted to the New York Etching Club. They were unanimously accepted for exhibit and hung without demur. They were awarded a high meed of praise, and such was the enthusiasm elicited that the unknown artist was elected a member of the organization.

When the members of the New York Etching Club were invited to send examples of their work to the newly formed "Royal Society of Painter-Etchers" of London, England, whose President was that prince of English Etchers, Seymour Haden, she with a number of others of the New York Club were elected members and received their diplomas signed by Queen Victoria herself.

As the etchings were simply signed M. Nimmo (her maiden name), she was supposed to be a man and for years was addressed as such in communications from the London Society. For many years no other woman was admitted.

At the Chicago Columbian Exposition in 1893 she was awarded a diploma and medal for her exhibit of etchings. The salient characteristics of Mrs. Moran's style were her striking originality, the broad treatment of her subject, combined with boldness of execution and entire immunity from affectation.

Mrs. Moran's favorite studio was beneath the spreading boughs of some hospitable tree, and the broad face of nature supplied her with grand and ever-beautiful subjects which were mirrored with the utmost fidelity in the sheet of copper—which with her supplied the place of the painter's canvas.

This mode of work, while possessing many obvious advantages over reproductions, would necessarily present almost insurmountable difficulties to a person not well versed in the technicalities of art. In copying a picture, all the points are clearly elucidated by the painter, and the etcher has only to follow with mechanical precision the interpretation of the artist. Nature is not always a safe guide to the uninitiated, and the etcher from nature must be endowed with a quick eye and a just appreciation of values and tones and half-tones. A line once bitten is not as easily effaced as one made by the pencil, nor can any mistake be covered with one deft stroke of the colorist's brush. The beauty of an etching lies in its autographic expression, even the very irregularities of an etched line possessing a certain fascination to connoisseurs.

In the long list of original etchings produced by Mrs. Moran, every one without exception was drawn on the plate directly from nature. Mrs. Moran was noted for her intense personality and freedom from conventionalism. She was a most able exponent of rural scenes, and in her treatment of foliage she aimed at forms rather than masses.

Nor was she an erratic artist, as is the case with many persons of genius, but a systematic and industrious worker, the number and variety of her conceptions showing enthusiasm and concentration in her art.

At the Spring Exhibition of the work of the women etchers of America to the Union League Club of New

York, Mrs. Moran contributed fifty-eight examples, some of them being very large. Several plates measured twenty by thirty inches.

"East Hampton Barrens" is interesting, both from its intrinsic merit and also as being one of the four original etchings made in 1879. Some of Mrs. Moran's experimental plates were considered by competent judges to equal in excellence many of her later works. The one mentioned is instinct with meaning, and the magic touch of the artist's hand has transmuted into poesy what would otherwise have been rather a commonplace subject.

"Twilight" in Scotch tone and roulette has the peculiarly soft effects incident to the method of etching. The gray night is succeeding the glow with which the setting sun has glorified the landscape, a hush pervades all nature, and the dark masses of trees are outlined dimly against the fading sky. All is peace, rest, sublime quietude.

"A Goose Pond, East Hampton, Long Island" is the diploma etching which gained the etcher admission to the ranks of the Royal Society of Painter-Etchers of London. The placid water reveals depth and surface and the effects of light and aerial space are extremely well managed.

"Between the Gloaming and the Murk" is an idyllic pastoral, beautifully expressed in soft tints of monochrome. This is etched in line with mezzotint. A purple twilight haze suffuses the quiet scene; even the slow lazy pace of the cows winding their way homeward is suggestive of silence and tranquility, while the hush of eventide broods over the dying landscape. This etching was published by Cassell & Co. in "Twenty Etchings by Noted Americans." It is one of the artist's most tender and dreamy conceptions.

The "Home Sweet Home" of John Howard Payne shows the gable-end of the old house so dear to the writer of the song and so well depicted in the etching.

"While through the willows creaking loud is heard the busy mill" is one of Mrs. Moran's largest plates, being twenty by thirty inches. It is also one of her *chefs-d'oeuvre.* The old mill is a picturesque object, reminding one of the Dutch scenes so dear to painters. The long shadows lie upon the grass and the gradations of light and shade are delicately yet strongly indicated. The sky values and tones have been consistently preserved and the homely beauty of the scene is replete with a delightful suggestiveness.

Among Mrs. Moran's later works are two Florida scenes, etched in 1887, during the artist's sojourn in Florida. "A Florida Forest" for its fidelity to nature and its minute attention to detail is unexcelled in its way; each leaf and branch presents a realistic picture. The woods are a tangled mass of tropical verdure, trailing vines and hanging parasites; above the dense undergrowth rise the feathery, fern-like palms, lifting their heads almost to the heavens, while the branches of the live-oak trees overshadow the pool of dark sluggish water, which sleeps calmly beneath the burning rays of the Southern sun.

Quite in a different style is another Florida scene, "Point Isabel, Coast of Florida." Scarcely a tree or shrub shades the solitary spot and the barren wave-washed strand presents the appearance of supreme desolation. Treated by a less skilled hand, the scene would be tiresome, monotonous, and lacking in interest. Instead, it bears the stamp of originality and is imbued with a strong poetic sentiment. By connoisseurs it is classed among the most finished works of Mrs. Moran. It would be impossible in a short article to chronicle Mrs. Moran's numerous etchings but it suffices to say that in this line of art she stands preeminent among her sister etchers, both in this country and abroad.

In social life Mrs. Moran was a charming woman and a bright and graceful conversationalist; she was thoroughly conversant with the different phases of art. Her personnel was just the type one expects to see in a woman of artistic temperament, her face indicating distinct individuality and great intelligence. The abundant dark hair was softened by a sprinkling of gray over her broad forehead, and beneath were expressive dark gray eyes which lighted up with enthusiasm when she talked on a subject that interested her. Mrs. Moran was of medium height, erect and, though a little inclined to embonpoint, had a graceful figure and dressed with a peculiar quaintness that was a part of the simple charm of her character. She was as modest and unassuming and as free from ostentation and affectation as gifted natures usually are. As a wife, mother, homemaker, neighbor and friend, she possessed all the qualities that make for happiness and brighten life. A rounded character, perfect in its naturalness and simplicity, she died while still full of interest and work of all kinds; too early, it seemed, but she had lived much and worked much, and was more tired than she knew, and so rested early.

To other women workers, she was a living proof that, at least in artistic work, if one's mind and heart are large enough for both, there can be the great happiness of home making and intellectual work combined.

WITH MORAN

IN THE YELLOWSTONE

WILLIAM HENRY JACKSON *

MY ACQUAINTANCE with Thomas Moran dates from 1871, when he accompanied the Hayden Geological Survey on the first official exploration of the Yellowstone country. As the official photographer of the expedition my duties brought us much together during the trip—the beginning of a life-long friendship and of many other outings, including the Yellowstone again, in the Rocky Mountain regions. The memory of that first one, however, is the most precious and in the following pages I will relate, as well as memory serves my purpose, the story of that memorable

* From Appalachia, September, 1938. The author was still active as a traveler, camper, artist, and author, at the age of 94 when he wrote this article. He died at the age of 99.

journey with him into the newly discovered but still mysterious wilderness of the Northwest. I have very little material, I am sorry to say, for the details of daily travel and camp life. I was not a diarist at the time, nor was Moran, and while the main events of that period are still well remembered, the friendly gossip that goes on around the camp fire, with other familiar incidents of such an experience, have passed almost entirely out of mind.

Yellowstone, here, means all that mountainous region up in northwestern Wyoming known as the Yellowstone National Park, the first, largest and most remarkable of all our national playgrounds. It was long a remote region of myth and legend among mountain men and their kind, the subject of many fantastic conceptions that for a long time were not taken seriously.

Government first became interested in the matter when Raynolds, engaged in exploration of the upper Missouri and Yellowstone country in 1859-60, was ordered to discover the sources of Yellowstone River and to trace it through lake and canyons out to the plains. Making the attempt too early in the season from the headwaters of Wind River, he was balked by impassable snows. Posterity has much to be thankful for that he did not succeed.

Dr. Hayden, who was to make the first official survey of that same region twelve years later, was a member of the Raynolds Expedition, as was old Jim Bridger, said to know more about all that country than anyone else, and who, no doubt, was expecting to declare "I told you so" about some of his own marvellous stories should the expedition pass that way.

The discovery of gold in Alder Gulch, near Virginia City, Montana, in 1863, brought a rush of prospectors from all over the country who penetrated every nook and cranny of the upper Yellowstone region. Some of them, undoubtedly, at one time or another in their wanderings, saw more or less of its remarkable features as did the old fur trappers before their time; but they were interested only in locating a good prospect and paid little attention to anything, however wonderful it might be, where a few "colors" could not be panned out from the gravels of its water courses.

But interest was increasing with settlement of adjacent regions and eventually a few enterprising and adventurous citizens of Montana decided that they must find out how much of truth there was in all this talk about "Colter's Hell," a mountain of clear glass, and marvellous petrifactions, too wonderful to be believed without investigation. Two parties were organized for this purpose, one of which, the so-called Washburn-Langford Expedition of 1870, was the more efficient in number engaged, character of personnel and information obtained. The publicity given to the world at large by its returning members created general interest throughout the country, stimulated by N.P. Langford, particularly, through illustrated articles in Scribners Magazine * and by lectures throughout the country.

---

* The Wonders of the Yellowstone, by N. P. Langford, Scribners Monthly Magazine, May-June, 1871.

Dr. Hayden, of course, was profoundly interested in these developments relating so closely to his own experiences. Although prepared for the continuation of the work of his organization in other localities, he decided, after attending Langford's lecture in Washington, January 19, 1871, to make the Yellowstone, instead, the field of his operations for the current season.

Just how Moran happened to accompany the expedition is not a matter of record, and is chiefly conjectural. He had prepared some of the illustrations for Langford's articles in Scribners Magazine. The illustrations, themselves, were of no particular importance but as the first of their kind ever to appear in print were of more than ordinary interest at the time. The romance, however, surrounding the discovery of so much that was marvellous in nature's handiwork must have appealed strongly to Moran's lively imagination and to a determination to see for himself the wonders he had been called upon to depict in terms of his art. He was not in affluent circumstances at the time but the proceeds of a loan on one of his best paintings furnished the means with which to make the all important adventure.

The expedition, consisting of some thirty-five persons as it left the rendezvous camp at Ogden, Utah, reached Virginia City, Montana, early in July. This well known and one time notorious mining camp of the early sixties had little left of its former prosperity. The nearby placers, that had furnished its wealth of golden nuggets, were now practically "played out,"

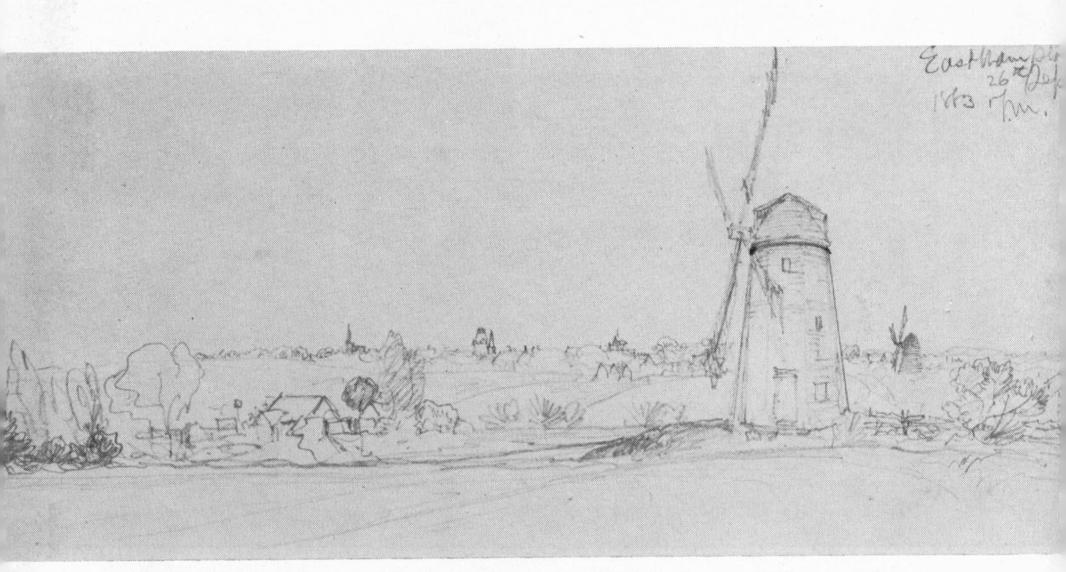

"East Hampton, Sept. 26th, 1883." Two pencil sketches by Thomas Moran.

"Twilight, East Hampton, L. I." Etching by Mary Nimmo Moran. 1880.

A leaf from the Moran Guest Book.

4.

Dear Madame

In answer to you questions

I was born in Strathaven, Scotland in 1842 Coming to America while still a Child when sixteen years of age I met my husband Thomas Moran, ~~the~~ well known landscape painter then well known as an Artist and from him came all my first impressions of Art and of Nature as applied to Art; up to that time I had never thought of ~~applying~~ using the my ~~self~~ brush or pencil. We were married in 1862 and from that time on I may say I have always been my Husbands pupil. I often painted landscape in Water Color but nothing of importance then in Oil exhibiting in the

Autobiographical note, in handwriting of Mary Nimmo Moran.

24 West 22nd st
New York
Jan 29th/1901

Mr — Nicholson
My dear Sir.
Since the reseipt of Your letter (in regard to an Article on the Grand Canon from the Artists Point of view) I have mislaid it, & hoping to find it have delayed reply. Although I would like to serve the Co in the manner suggested, after thinking it over, & trying it on, I have decided that my literary capacity is "Nil". I tried it once before, & on re reading the Article in the Century Magazine I felt Ashamed of it, & have re resolved not to again take pen in hand for publication. I am of opinion that nothing finer or more descriptive of the Grand Canon ~~can be written~~ (for those who have not seen it) can be written, than the one done by our dear dead friend Higgins After the trip we made there together.

While I wish that I had literary Capasity to give to others what I see in the Grand Canon, I am Convinced that I can only paint it, which I expect to Continue to do until my hand ceases to work.

Yours Very Sincerely
T. Moran.

A letter by Thomas Moran.

Illustration for "An Island of the Sea"
Scribner's Magazine September 1878.

Pen and Ink sketch.

Mount Moran and, to the right of the mountain, Moran Canyon. Grand Teton National Park, Wyoming. Photograph by Crandall

but it was still the wide-open and ramshackle "city" of a mining camp and afforded amusement or excitement, as the case might be, for anyone who looked for it. Moran first joined the party here, overtaking it by a five-day journey by stage coach from Ogden over the route that had been followed by the expedition.

He was 34 years old at this time, of slight and frail physique, and did not seem to be of the kind to endure the strenuous life of the wilderness. But he was wiry and active in getting about and keenly enthusiastic about his participation in the work of the expedition. He had never camped out before except for a night's bivouac on the shore of Lake Superior ten years previous. This was his first experience in Rocky Mountain regions, coming out entirely unacquainted with his associates or with the country itself and all that related to it. But he made the adventure with fine courage and quickly adapted himself to the new and unfamiliar conditions and, as it turned out later, none was more untiring on the trail or less mindful of unaccustomed food or hard bed under a little shelter tent, than he was. At home fastidious and careful of his diet, with a strong aversion to fats, he wrote in one of his letters about camp life "You should see me bolt the bacon."

His personal equipment was simple like that of everyone else, little attention being given to special outing costumes for the occasion. Flannel shirts and heavy boots, into which trousers were tucked, were the mainstay, with overcoat and blanket roll as a necessary adjunct. Moran had never ridden a horse before, and while getting accustomed to this experience was quite unabashed in using his camp pillow to protect his rather spare anatomy from the hard lines of a McClellan saddle. But, despite his lack of horsemanship, he made a picturesque appearance when mounted. The jaunty tilt of his sombrero, long yellowish beard, and portfolio under his arm marked the artistic type, with something of local color imparted by a rifle hung from saddle horn.

At Fort Ellis, a military cantonment garrisoned by a battalion of the 2d U. S. Cavalry, a few days were spent in outfitting with pack animals. Wagons had been used for the transportation of camp equipment and supplies to this point, but for the rest of the way into the wilderness beyond, that had never been marked by a wagon track, they must be left behind.

Another expedition for the exploration of the Yellowstone country came into Fort Ellis along with the Hayden party. It was sent out by the War Department under the direction of Captains Barlow and Heap, U. S. Corps of Engineers. It was not as large a party as Hayden's, but an escort of a company of cavalry (ostensibly for the benefit of both parties) was detailed to accompany it so that their number was materially increased. Nearly all of this escort, however, was soon recalled for more serious duty elsewhere.

The engineers and the escort got off first. Hayden's expedition followed a day later, taking the wagons over a rather hard road to Botelers Ranch on the Yellowstone where the transfer to packs was made. Two or three days were required to make the change, with trouble enough, the first day out on the trail, from obstreperous, bucking mules and slipping packs. But these difficulties were soon forgotten in the more orderly routine that was soon established.

For two or three days the trail lay along the river, with lofty mountain ranges on either side, sometimes crossing small level spaces but more often climbing over rocky ledges that compressed the stream into cascades through narrow gorges. As an introduction to mountainous Yellowstone beyond, the landscape effects seen in water, trees and mountains offered many opportunities for the work of both artist and photographer. The photography of this period, by the way, was quite a different affair from what it is today with its miniature cameras and prepared films. For this expedition a pack-mule load of apparatus and materials was required, and also the services of one or two assistants for its practice. This comprised the preparation of plates in an extemporized "dark room" and development at once after exposure in the camera. These operations were of more or less interest in the party generally, and frequently volunteer assistants accompanied the photographer just to see how it was done. Moran was particularly interested in this part of the survey's business, and was always one of the little party that lingered behind or wandered far afield to portray the picturesque or remarkable along the way.

Mammoth Hot Springs, first of Yellowstone's wonders to be encountered on the trail, had not been seen by the explorers of the year before. Known only by men of the mountains, trappers, prospectors, or Indians, it was reserved for the present expedition to rediscover them, as it were, and put them on the map as one of the remarkable features of the region.

The engineers named them "The Soda Springs." Hayden, in his first report, called them the "White Mountain Hot Springs." Seen from a distance that was one's first impression of them. But this first view of snow white deposits, terracing the mountain side for more than a square mile, thousands of feet from summit to base, gave little indication of the beauty in form and color of its separate features, steaming springs, whose waters deposited lines of brilliant color in flowing over the formations. This was a wonderful revelation of contrast and color for Moran, who transferred much of its detail to the beautiful water color sketches that have recently been acquired by the National Park Service. He was also as interested as the photographer himself in selecting the view points for each negative, having in mind, perhaps, the good use he could make of the photographs later in some of his own compositions.

A motor car now makes the distance between Mammoth Hot Springs and Tower Falls, over a modern highway, in less than an hour. The expedition, following an old trail wherever it could be found, was the best part of two days in doing it; but there were fine views to be had along this part of the river and canyon not to be enjoyed by more rapid means of travel. Around Tower Falls also the scenery is worth more than the casual look-over it generally gets. The weird and fantastic towers and pinnacles along the turbulent creek above the falls contrast strangely with the chaste beauty of the Hot Springs and caught Moran's fancy. He had made some singular pictures, from description, of these rocks for Langford's article and naturally was greatly interested in getting his own interpretation of their picturesque and varied outlines.

The way had been blazed through this wonderland by the Washburn expedition in naming and describing the chief points of interest; but they had followed the dim traces of former trails—game, Indian or white man's—that passed to the sources of the Yellowstone and then over to the southern water shed. This trail was picked up here and there and followed by the pack train, as far as possible, but most of the party, on investigation bent, wandered far and wide, and it happened occasionally that some of them had a hard time locating camp at nightfall.

There was some rough traveling between Tower Falls and the canyon, passing Mt. Washburn on the way; some went around its eastern base, others over the top for the bird's eye view of the entire lake basin and the canyon, but the larger number went by the pass to the west and then followed a tortuous trail to make camp on a small creek near the canyon and falls. It was early afternoon of a perfect day when they arrived, and the view was at its best. There was little time for silent contemplation of its grandeur and beauty, for the train was to move on in the morning and there was much work to do.

Moran's enthusiasm was greater here than anywhere else among Yellowstone's wonderful features. Studying the view from each vantage point on the rim of the canyon and sometimes from its depths, I imagine he carried away in his mind more of its marvelous color and varied forms than he put into his sketches, as well as the conviction, it would seem, that here was something peculiarly adapted to his own remarkable technique as a painter and fit subject for a masterpiece.

"It is not strange that this canyon has been a theme for writer, painter and photographer, from its discovery to the present time. But at first thought it is strange that all attempts to portray its beauties are less satisfactory than those pertaining to any other feature of the Park. . . . The artist Moran acknowledged that 'its beautiful tints were beyond the reach of human art.' And General Sherman said of this celebrated artist's effort: 'The painting by Moran is good, but painting and words are unequal to the subject.' " *

The reference here is to Moran's first large painting of the canyon, hanging in one of the corridors of the Capitol at Washington. Since its purchase by the Government it has been shamefully neglected and all but ruined by attempts at cleaning or restoration. A larger and more recent painting of the same subject by him, in the National Art Gallery, is the product of his matured experience as a painter of the Yellowstone, and more nearly represents what even he thought was "beyond the reach of human art."

Never since their formation in remote ages had the cliffs over-looking canyon and falls seen such stirring

---

* The Yellowstone National Park, by H. M. Chittenden, Captain, Corps of Engineers, United States Army. Third Edition, 1900.

times as in those latter days of July, 1871. The engineers and numerous escort had measured and sounded all the depths and heights and photographed from the best points of view. When the Hayden Expedition came straggling in from over and around Mt. Washburn each and every one, after a brief period of wonder and amazement, spread all over the formation from Inspiration Point to the Upper Falls. Besides its own photographer the survey was accompanied by another one, J. Crissman, of Bozeman, Montana, as a guest for this occasion. With photographic equipment of dark boxes and tents set up under the trees bordering the canyon, plate after plate was made from every available point of view.

But that is not the whole story. J. T. Hine, photographer for the Engineers, returned to Chicago with his precious negatives just in time to have them all destroyed, before printing, in the Great Fire of that year. Crissman's work was cut short by the loss of his camera, which, left unguarded for a moment, was blown over into the depths of the canyon, never to be recovered. Back in Washington, that winter of 1871-2, in the proceedings before Congress for the creation of the Yellowstone National Park, the water colors of Moran and the photographs of the Geological Survey were the most important exhibits brought before the Committee. "They did a work which no other agency could do and doubtless convinced every one who saw them that the regions where such wonders existed should be preserved to the people forever." *

* *Ibid,* H. M. Chittenden.

Beyond the canyon and falls into the more open spaces of Hayden Valley the river meandered placidly through grassy meadows with frequent vistas of snow-capped mountains. Here also were some of the amazingly strange displays of subterranean forces, sulphur springs, paint pots and mud geysers that were responsible for the short but suggestive name by which the region was first known. These features, while exciting in a way, were of less interest to Moran, from the number of sketches made, than were the landscape effects that included the lake as seen from its outlet, with its dots of wooded islands and background of the Absarokas.

There was a separation of the two parties at the lake, the Engineers turning to the left and the Hayden Survey to the right to follow its shore lines; while the military part of the expeditions returned to Fort Ellis. The western side of the lake is a wooded wilderness without trails, but, traveling sometime along the beach and then through the timber, camp was made finally at its extreme western arm among the paint pots and steaming pools. From here quick trips were made by small parties over to the Geyser Basins. Moran joined the photographic party as one of them in making it. Without chart, landmark or guide, and with great uncertainty as to direction or distance, some of the toughest traveling conditions of the entire season were encountered. Thick growths of jack pines, wide swaths of down timber from wind-falls, and almost impassable ravines, tried the patience and endurance of all alike. By good luck the Fire Hole River was struck near the geysers in the Upper Basins. But, less than two days was all the time that could be devoted to that wonderful region, from Old Faithful to the Excelsior, for a quick return must be made to the lake camp to rejoin the expedition in extending its exploration around the lake.

Moran left the expedition here, going out with a small party that returned to the base camp at Botelers for supplies. With sketch books and portfolios, and also memory, stored with abundant material he was eager to get back to his studio and begin working on those wonderful creations that were to bring fame and fortune in the years to follow.

THOMAS MORAN, N.A., THE GRAND OLD MAN OF AMERICAN ART

GUSTAVE H. BUEK *

I FIRST MET Thomas Moran in the Summer of 1892. I had been commissioned by the Santa Fe Railway to reproduce by lithography his painting of The Grand Canyon of Arizona, one of the conditions being that the reproduction before acceptance should be endorsed as satisfactory by the artist. Knowing Moran to have done some excellent lithographing himself, as well as being master of practically all the then known reproductive methods, I naturally approached him with considerable hesitation. No man could have received a younger man with greater cordiality than he received me.

* Excerpts from article in The Mentor, August, 1924.

Through my visits at the National Academy and Water Color Society Exhibitions at the old Academy at the corner of 23rd Street and Fourth Avenue, New York City, I had, before this, become acquainted with the work both in oil and water-color of Moran, and had early been drawn to it by his remarkable draughtsmanship and feeling for color. To my mind he stood far in advance of most of his contemporaries.

During the years following that first meeting at his charming home in the old village of East Hampton, Long Island, I enjoyed many opportunities for companionship with the artist and for close observation of his work.

While he does not belong to the accepted school of impressionism, he nevertheless is an impressionist. "What I ask," he says, "is to see a man's brains as evidenced in his work. I want to know what his opinions are. He is the arbiter of his own pictures and nature. Zola's definition of art exactly fills my demands when he said 'Art is nature seen through a temperament.' . . . An artist's business is to produce for the spectator of his pictures the impression produced by nature on himself."

Mr. Moran always upheld the importance of fidelity in detail in producing Nature—a fidelity that can only be achieved by fullness of knowledge. In the painting of a landscape, a thorough knowledge of the formation of clouds, of rocks, of trees, of the ground itself and all that it holds, is necessary.

"In art, as in any other profession," Mr. Moran maintained, "knowledge is power. Twist this in any form you may, it remains a truth, and the foundation stone of all art. It will always be the same, and will always show itself in the pictures of the artist, no matter how humble, or how pretentious. Just how far the artist shall go with his knowledge is left to him. He must typify his own personality. This covers all—taste, opinions, everything. The man must exhibit himself in his pictures. This is the theory of art, and also of judgement. Knowledge in art is the power behind the handwork. Eyesight is nothing unless backed by brains. In condensed form this is my theory of art. In painting I have to be full of my subject. I have to have knowledge. I must know the rocks and the trees, and the atmosphere and the mountain torrents, and the birds that fly in the blue ether above us. Whatever of arbitrary forms that grow out of this intimacy with nature becomes a part of the work is altogether legitimate because my knowledge of the topic leads me to take liberties."

As was once said of one of the great masters of the Barbizon School, "There is something deeply serious and sensitive in his soul, which made him a fit instrument for the rendering of those grand harmonies of Nature's more dramatic side. Thoroughly saturated with a love for art—endowed with a positive and original genius, with an intense love of nature and a sensitiveness to her more delicate beauty, all nature was grand, and revealed to him her most poetic side. Serene, calm, and joyous, he painted the beauty about him with deep devotion to nature, to which he was thoroughly attuned.

"He absorbed the beauty of all her many moods, and with a devotion that was never surpassed gave his life to the placing upon canvas the lessons learned from her. He did not try to make her conform to a preconceived idea of what art should be, but painted the beautiful impressions that the subject gave him. There is always the freshness of nature in his pictures."

Every word of the above can truthfully be said of Thomas Moran. No painter was ever more conscientious in his work than he; none more devoted in spirit, none more uncompromising in integrity.

He does not like to be called "The Scientist Artist"; he frankly admits that his is not the scientific mind, that masters and retains—that carefully stores up for future reference and use the visible facts in nature. But he has a marvelous memory that holds these facts, ever ready at his command, as I have had many occasions of observing. I know of no other artist whose work, while done in love of all that is great and beautiful in nature, is yet so thoroughly correct in a scientific sense as the landscape painting of Thomas Moran. His mind seems to be a sensitive plate on which every phenomenon in nature has been impressed.

And how varied in subject is his work; how marvelously many-sided is Moran in all he does! He is equally at home whether painting the superb scenery of the Rockies, the Grand Canyon of Arizona, or the Yellowstone, the Yosemite Region, the tropical scenery of Florida or of Old Mexico, the quiet, restful stretches of Eastern Long Island, or the peaceful pastoral scenery of England. Again, we see the master touch in his paintings of the enchanting canals and fairy-like architecture of Venice, and the grandeur of the ocean in her stormiest moods, when wave and sky combine to challenge the artist's skill.

Generally speaking, he is a patient worker, and while quick to conceive or select a subject, he is conscientiously deliberate in carrying it out. And not infrequently, as the mood or a sudden impulse strikes him, he completely changes his subject when half finished. I have known him to change a carefully constructed snow-capped mountain range into a raging storm at sea; the formations of the mountains suddenly giving him the sense and feeling of white-crested waves with their heights and depths. These ocean scenes, of which he did not paint many, are eagerly sought after.

No painting ever left his easel that was not considered by him to be the very best that he could do at the time, and none that was not considered by him as "finished." He is incapable of slighting or misrepresenting a fact, incapable of doing what he does not feel to be just to his art and to himself. Thoroughly honest and sincere in his art, as in his life! On one occasion I took a friend, who was not especially an admirer of the work of Moran, to his studio in 22nd Street, New York City, and we found him working on a half-finished painting of a Western scene. The subject had been boldly laid in in broad masses and looked quite different from one of his finished paintings. My friend was captivated by the work in that state, and, taking me aside, asked me to persuade Moran to leave the canvas exactly as it was, and sign it; adding that he would gladly pay the price that Moran would ask for it when it was finished.

This request I communicated to Moran. He declined absolutely, saying that the painting, as it was, was not correct as to geological facts and consequently could not leave his studio in that state. Another example of his insistence that his painting must have his own complete endorsement before leaving his hands was when a prospective buyer (a collector having one of the finest collections of paintings in the country, and a man of enormous means) offered to purchase "The Shoshone Falls," one of Moran's great paintings, at the price asked ($15,000.00) if he would change the character of the sky. This he refused to do, although urged to do so by his friend, Hopkinson Smith. In consequence, he lost the sale—which was preferable to him to losing the feeling of locality imparted by the sky as originally painted.

Such incidents show the sincerity of the man.

Since my first meeting with Thomas Moran, I have had occasion to spend many hours with him, both in travel in the Far West and in his studio and home, as well as in my home; and while I regret that I cannot clearly recall the many interesting talks with him on art, travel and literature, and must consequently rely largely on interviews in which he has expressed himself to others as well as to me, still I hope to convey a slight idea of the man and his attitude toward a subject that has engrossed his entire active life, and that still today, in his eighty-eighth year, when he has practically laid aside his brush and palette, and while still in good health and spirits, is his constant thought—The Art Movement in America by American Artists.

In an interview some years ago Moran made this statement as to his adoption of America as the field of his operations: "I decided very early that I would be an American painter. I'll paint as an American, on an American basis, and American only. I traveled the country over and the West appealed to me. I like the comparatively flat land of Eastern Long Island, such as I have near my studio at East Hampton and Montauk; and then I like the rugged mountains of the Rockies."

Moran's earlier work, at times, shows a multiplicity of detail, often to an inordinate degree, but this was at a time when he was the careful and conscientious student of every fact in nature that would or might add to the interest of his subject. As his work broadened, this knowledge of details was most valuable, enabling him to introduce them at will and yet subordinate them so that they, in nowise, interfered with or disturbed the general effect. This knowledge of detail was especially valuable to him in painting his great pictures of the Far West, where flora and fauna are an important and essential part of the scene depicted. In writing this, I recall the remark made to me by one of our foremost artists when looking across the Grand Canyon on a remarkably clear day: "How I could paint this, if I only had Moran's knowledge!"

Moran's work throughout his entire life suggests refinement. Refinement is the key-note. It is found in his painting of the architecture of Venice, and of its brilliantly picturesque life on the Canals; it is found in his painting of the great snowcapped mountain ranges of the Rockies, and in the colorful buttes and mesas of New Mexico and Arizona. Always refinement, born of and backed by knowledge, and yet never sacrificing vigor of drawing.

The versatility of the man is amazing, and can be accounted for only by the fact that his knowledge of the component parts necessary to the construction of his pictures is so thorough that he is never at a loss for original compositions.

His studies from nature are very carefully made, almost without exception in water-colors, and if found necessary, supplemented by accurate drawings in pencil or wash. The facts noted in these studies become so firmly fixed in his mind that he needs seldom to refer to them when painting his pictures.

Those that have been fortunate enough to go with him over the hundreds of sketches in water-color and in black and white—the results of many trips made by him during his long and busy life—have enjoyed an experience never to be forgotten.

Notable among the sketches are those of the Rio Virgin in Utah, and of the Grand Canyon made in 1873. These first sketches of that part of our country, which are the art means of bringing the grandeur and beauty of that Far Western scenery to the American people, have a value all their own. It is pleasant to know that Moran has presented many of these sketches to the Cooper Institute in New York City for the benefit of the art students of that institution.

His travels took him not only into our Great Western

Country but also into Florida, Mexico and the West Indies as well, and extended throughout Europe, especially into Italy and England, in all of which places he found material for paintings. His well-known painting of "Mount Moran" in the Teton Range, "The Mountain of the Holy Cross" in Colorado, his great historical landscape "Ponce de Leon in Florida," and his paintings full of the dreamy beauty of Venice, are but a few of the outstanding results of these trips.

And now, in his eighty-eighth year, after seventy years of active studious work, knowing that his great work is done, standing at the twilight of his life, he has the great satisfaction of knowing that, in the integrity of his character and the sincerity of his work, he has added beauty to the world and value to American art.

A MORAN CENTENARY

FRANK WEITENKAMPF *

THOMAS MORAN was born in 1837. The centenary of that event is marked by the Library's Prints Division in an exhibition of prints by this artist, open during February.

Thomas Moran made experiments in etching as early as 1857, but his most noteworthy work on copper was produced in the late 'seventies and 'eighties, in the period of the old New York Etching Club. His definite, clean-cut draftsmanship, as well as his qualities as a painter, had their influence on, and a decided reflection in, his etched work. Critics have spoken of his nervous vitality, boldness in conception, vigor in execution, indication of color effect.

His tendency to paint the grandly picturesque, shown in paintings such as those of Venice and of the Yellowstone, is quite as apparent in a number of his

* From Bulletin of the New York Public Library, February, 1937.

prints—for example in the sunny "Gate of Venice" or the sombre lithograph "Solitude." But he could also turn to the simpler aspects of nature and present them in intimate bits such as "An Old Apple Orchard, Easthampton," "A Bit of Old Jersey," or "In the Newark Meadows." In the last he quietly emphasizes the unobtrusive beauties of those swampy stretches past which many ride daily, unseeing. Yet even here he was apt, as in "Hook Pond, Easthampton," to expand an unassuming landscape into the sweep of the grand manner, the picturesque effect, though without departing from essential facts.

Everything seemed to attract him: the swirl of clouds, towering cliffs, trees (he made studies of apple trees, buttonwoods, willows), the "much resounding sea," the rockbound coast, sand dunes, water meadows.

His Turner-like qualities are familiar, and in fact he reproduced paintings by that artist ("Conway Castle") and by others, including himself. The choice of subject in his original etchings at times carries faint reminder of other artists. Of Constable, for instance, in "A Rustic Bridge"; of Hayden, in "An English River." In one of his small early lithographs, done around 1860, he recalls Eugene Isabey, for whose bravura effects he presents more subdued, though rich, tones.

He worked with various media, in etching adapting technique to need, as when he drew waves in widely spaced lines ("The Lighthouse"), a little in the manner of our present-day C. H. Woodbury. He could turn from the blond lightness of "Castle of San Juan, Vera

Cruz" to the dark richness of "Harlech Castle," with a slight suggestion of Turner's "Liber Studiorum," done in etching and mezzotint. The latter combination he used repeatedly. He courted the lithographic stone when lithography for artists was not a live issue in this country. He even tried the "glass cliché" process used in France by Corot and others. In all of this one hardly gets the feeling of experimentation. It seems a matter of intention fully carried out with easy sureness.

It is that mastery of technique to get the desired effect that forms much of the interest of these prints. They speak of a time when a group of American artists were bravely active in the cause of original etching, when there were even some attempts at painter-lithography. And they are not without their lesson of sound craftsmanship for artists of today, no matter how little or how much the latter may depart from the ideals and standards here exemplified.

THE WATER-COLORS OF THOMAS MORAN

ROBERT ALLERTON PARKER *

THE RECENT retrospective exhibition of Thomas Moran's water-colors shown in New York has done much to revive interest in the more intimate aspects of an artist of the nineteenth century to whom all Americans owe an immense debt of gratitude, and whose influence upon our culture is only now beginning to be dimly realized. Modernistic critics may scoff because Moran remained blandly unconscious of the technique of a Cézanne or a Renoir. But, fortunately, there are several ways in which a painter may be creative; and despite the limitations of his method, Thomas Moran may be honestly acclaimed as a creative artist.

As Marcel Proust has pointed out in that encyclo-

* Excerpts from article in International Studio, March, 1927.

pedic novel of his (it is, incidentally, an admirable manual of aesthetics), each truly creative artist compels us to look at the external world through his own eyes. He re-creates the world of Nature anew for each spectator. The artist is in a sense, says Proust, a sort of oculist who treats our eyes. The treatment is painful, until at last it is as though he exclaimed, "Now look!" and it is as though some geological upheaval had taken place. Such an artist reigns in our consciousness until a new one comes along to re-create Nature again for us.

In this sense Thomas Moran was creative. He opened the eyes of Americans to the vast inexhaustible expanses of natural beauty upon our own continent. He was a pioneer like the other argonauts of his time; but he went forth in search of beauty as others were in search of copper, gold and oil. He was creative because he awakened the American consciousness to the permanent value of those wide, measureless expanses of wilderness, of sky and mountain and extravagances of Nature, as natural resources of beauty, to be prized and conserved and held as great national parks. In the slang of our own day, Moran's canvases exerted a great influence in "selling" the idea of the Yellowstone National Park to the American people. More than any other artist, declares Stephen Tyng Mather, director of the National Park Service of the Department of the Interior, he made us acquainted with the great West. He was a "visualizer," the most persuasive herald, as Frederick W. Eddy has asserted, of that movement which has become popular under the title of "see America first."

Without attempting to demean or to minimize the effort of the great European iconoclasts who have re-created landscape painting by innovations in technique, it is high time that we recognize the achievement of our own Moran. At this particular moment, when so many of the younger American artists are working as in a vacuum, producing precious hothouse products so narrow in appeal as to interest only their sycophants and flatterers, these spontaneous water-colors of Thomas Moran brought the spectator anew to an appreciation of the gallant, adventurous, romantic gesture of the pioneer spirit of our own heroic age which has suffered by lack of appreciation.

One was surprised and delighted to find here the intimate Moran, an artist exquisite in sensibility and a veritable master in his analysis of the scattered heterogeneous elements of a vast expanse of wild nature into its essential elements, and the re-creation of these elements into a significant unit. "Color-notes" they might be called; and yet, after half a century, they live undimmed by the passage of time. They date less than the great canvases worked up, with how painstaking an effort, in the studio of the artist. Even more than the more pretentious products so industriously completed in his studio, the true connoisseur must cherish these bits of biographical art into which Thomas Moran poured his passionate adoration of wild nature.

These water-colors presented a vivid pictorial record of Thomas Moran's "prospecting" for the beauties of wild nature on the American continent. The Yellowstone water-colors were his effort to capture the hitherto unrecorded beauty of the Yellowstone in its every aspect, memoranda for the creation of the great paintings he imagined, and which later became realities. There were no less than fifteen of these sketches in the recent exhibition. All suggestive, accurate, effective as working plans, and accomplished with a precision in craftsmanship and a sober respect for detail, indicated by the marginal pencil notes, these Yellowstone sketches reveal graphically Thomas Moran's appreciation of the new universe of natural beauty which had been revealed to his eyes for the first time, and the exultance and ecstasy they awakened in his soul.

That expedition to the Yellowstone [in 1871] determined Moran's future career. For thirty years or more he ventured forth with pencil and brush to record his explorations and discoveries in the beauty of virgin nature. He liberated himself from the predominating influence of Turner—an influence evident in his earlier work—and created a type of landscape essentially American. For Moran no region was too inaccessible, too dangerous, provided it might provide a new thrill. We have the evidence of the recent exhibition to show that he discovered for himself the rugged majesty of Wyoming cliffs, the exotic extravagant color of Utah and the deserts of Nevada, the translucent limpidity of Lake Tahoe, of the Yosemite and New Mexico. Nor was he insensitive to the picturesque elements of such scenes as the smelters of Denver or the factories of Pittsburgh. Just as long before the advent of Paul Gauguin or Robert Louis Stevenson, Herman Melville in his novels had discovered the exotic beauty of the South Seas, so Thomas Moran has wandered down to New Mexico and Old, though a quarter of a century was to pass before the region around Taos and Santa Fe was to be rediscovered by contemporary artists.

The heroic gesture of the man lives in these water-colors. They are at once daring and modest. There is not discoverable in them the slightest evidence of preciosity. They suggest the joyous adventurous activity of a man who chose a continent for his playground. When the first series of Moran's Yellowstone water-colors were shown in 1874, an early admirer wrote of them: "Thomas Moran's water-colors show a strong man rejoicing to run a race, with all his senses alive for rich and strange and shimmering color. Rainbow and mist with fleeting cloud and more hues than iris, his love of form is as strong as his love of color; and his line betrays the same innate grace of spirit, the same delicately moving mind. . . ." These words remain as true today as when they were written.

Through the medium of these "notes" in water-color, the spirit of the valiant Thomas Moran is revealed to us of a generation that is sitting at the feet of younger idols. The man stands before us as authentically as Samuel Butler does in his letters. Moran loses nothing in artistic stature by this revelation. Irreverent by habit and nature as we have grown to be, with our much vaunted contempt for anything we can conveniently label as "Victorian," our respect for him increases. Yes, we must perforce concede that despite all the change of idiom wrought in the language of paint, despite the fact that the great oil-paintings of Thomas Moran have indeed "dated," even as have those of Dominique Ingres, he reappears in these modest water-color notes clothed in real dignity. They entitle him to a place among our native immortals, among the heroes of our golden age. They evoke a picture of an artist as authentic in his own field as Walt Whitman, David Thoreau or Herman Melville were in theirs. Surely it is not overpraise to suggest that Thomas Moran is worthy of a place in this heroic company.

Despite the prevalent passion for derogation, the fashion of undermining, through the medium of pseudobiography, all of the great reputations of the latter half of the nineteenth century, these men scale as of truly heroic stature against the pettiness of our younger generation. Our younger artists are too much concerned in petty experimentation. Men like Moran conceived the function of the artist in another manner. As artists they functioned in American society as members of this democracy, contributing to the life of the nation. Thomas Moran was neither disdainful nor conceited, nor ashamed to speak to his fellow-men in language they could understand. His finished canvases were not ends in themselves, but media through which beauty might be transmitted.

Of what significance, in the final analysis, is the fact or the possibility that even his most valued paintings may fade and pass irrevocably from the consciousness of America? His expression has passed into our very culture. Perhaps more than any other American painter of the latter half of the nineteenth century Thomas Moran compelled the American people to appreciate the beauty of its own continent, to look upon its wonders through his eyes, and to save these resources of natural beauty.

For in the tumult and shouting of contemporary criticism it is a truism too often forgotten that every aesthetic value we possess is not the result of chance, but has been created and expressed first of all by some pioneering artist and then repeated and reiterated until it has filtered through the consciousness of the nation and has become, gradually, a commonplace. Every idea of beauty is thus "conditioned" until finally its origin is forgotten or ignored. Without a Thomas Moran and such great venturers into the unexplored West, artists who succeeded in communicating to the American public at large their joy in the beauty of the Yellowstone, the Grand Canyon or of the Yosemite Valley, it is doubtful whether our great national parks would be in existence as such today. Who can say that they might not be prized only for such resources as they possessed in the way of imbedded copper, silver or gold, or as the source of great water-power? If only by this pragmatic test, Thomas Moran is entitled to be honored.

Nor can it be doubted that the younger generation of American artists might derive incalculable benefit if it could for a period give up its mood of introspection and self-analysis and, even at the risk of being condemned by the pseudo-modernists, become more interested in the objective universe; if it could, as Thomas Moran did, communicate to the public consciousness some of its own ecstasy and wonder and adoration of its marvels.